D1536408

KNOW ENGLISH EQUITATION AND TRAINING

Bruce and Sue Coen

Bill Weikel, Editor
THE FARNAM HORSE LIBRARY

HORSE LIBRARY

The Farnam Horse Library
8701 North 29th Street
Omaha, Nebraska 68112

FRONT COVER
Lon Lavery of Sharon Center, Ohio astride one of his favorite 5-gaited, Richlon Farm Saddlebreds. Photograph by Theodore Cogswell,

**PHOTOGRAPH
ACKNOWLEDGMENTS:**
Bruce and Sue Coen, Bonnie Coen of Horseplay Farm, Wooster, Ohio; Lon Lavery, Richlon Farm, Sharon Center, Ohio; Shelly Groom, Ed Tweed's Brusally Ranch, Scottsdale, Arizona; Theodore Cogswell, Staff Photographer, Farnam Companies, Inc.

CONTENTS

SECTION ONE — *Equitation For The English Rider*

SECTION TWO — *The Training Of The English Horse*

INTRODUCTION

KNOW ENGLISH EQUITATION
AND TRAINING

There are many kinds of horses and horsemen. There are also many kinds of horsemanship skills which have developed through the ages since man first decided to ride astride his horse, rather than aboard some device being pulled by it. These skills relate to a successful mode of communication between man and horse. The horse offers physical capacities far surpassing those possessed by his master, and man contributes the intellect required to direct their combined talents. Man *must* be able to successfully communicate with his horse.

In a sense, this same problem of "communication" exists between man and machinery. Machines can move mountains, zoom down roads at almost any speed desired, fly ten miles high, or dive several thousand feet beneath the surface of an ocean. Different kinds of machines are required, of course, but each has its dials to read and set, levers and pedals to push or pull, and perhaps wheels to turn. No matter their type and variety, man must know which to pull and push; and when and how much to do it. Once he has this skill, he can get the machine to do what he wants it to do. So it is with horses.

The point at issue, however, is the fact that the horse has many more "controls" than many people give him credit for. How these controls are developed and used depend upon the school of horsemanship being practiced. It is the purpose of this book to present *English* riding in a nutshell. It'll not be in depth, but it will present the essentials of this particular kind of equestrian effort.

The term "English" is a broad general term used much in the same way as one might use the word "airplane." There are various styles of airplanes, and there are various styles of English riding. These styles include the Hunt Seat, Forward Seat, Saddle Seat, Balanced Seat, and Dressage Seat. Each of these have much in common with the others, yet there are subtle differences.

There is no great mystique in learning to ride one of the seats of English type riding. All forms of horsemanship are basically the same. The small points of English equitation are not insurmountable obstacles for the Western rider who decides to learn one of the English seats. ■

3

SECTION ONE

EQUITATION FOR THE ENGLISH RIDER

CHAPTER ONE

THE ENGLISH HORSE — A BIT OF HISTORY

We often hear the terms "English" horse and "Western" horse. What do they mean? Is an English horse one imported from England? Is a Western horse from out West?

We must realize that when the horse was originally domesticated 1,400 years before Christ, saddles were unheard of. Many centuries later the Greeks began to ride on pads because they discovered how much more comfortable this was. About 300 A.D. the invention of stirrups attached to a girth revolutionized the use of the horse. Until this time man did not fight on horseback; he dismounted and met his opponent on foot. The stirrups made the rider's seat more secure and he could mount and dismount easily even when fully armed. He could even stand in his stirrups and reach further with his sword by having done so.

From this simple girth and stirrup arrangement, two basic types of saddles evolved. The first was designed for function. It was heavy and strong with a high pommel and cantle to hold the warrior in place during battle. The Western saddle, by way of the Spanish Conquistadores and Mexican Vaqueros, evolved from this saddle of the knights of old.

The second saddle was designed for comfort. It was a "civilian" saddle with a padded seat. The ladies and men not engaged in battle used this type of saddle. It eventually resembled what we think of as the park saddle of today. Federico Caprilli, an Italian riding master, varied the design to suit those horsemen who enjoyed hunting and jumping. This became known as the Forward Seat saddle.

The Conquistadores took the knights' saddle and narrowed the pommel so a rope could be wound around it. This became the Mexican horn as we know it. The familiar Western saddle was further modified from the Mexican Saddle.

And, as the two types of saddles evolved, so did two types of horses; the light horses and the draft horses. The draft horse was a powerfully built work animal that could do a good day's work but was not as speedy as his lighter brother the riding horse. The riding horse was more finely built, graceful and swift. The Arabian is the oldest of the light horse breeds. From him, through the Darley Arabian, Godolphin Arabian, and Byerly Turk, the English Thoroughbred had its origin. England's King Charles, who reigned from 1660 to 1685, is considered the initiator of this breed because it was through his interest and effort that these three great Arabian stallions were imported to England. The English Thoroughbred was not only a great race horse, he was also an excellent riding horse and hunter. These horses were ridden with the only style saddle familiar to the English people — the saddle we now call the English saddle.

When the immigrants to the New World rode horseback, these saddles were used. We must remember that most of the first immigrants were from England. It is also a fact that the first horses imported by these people were English Thoroughbreds. It was later that the Mexican saddle came into use by the Americans who moved further West.

As the Americans moved further South and West they came into contact with the wild mustangs, descendants of horses brought to Mexico by the Spanish Conquistadores. The mustangs could exist in the West better than their eastern counterparts, so were caught and broken. The Mexican saddle was used on them because it was a working saddle. These western men made their living rounding up cattle and wild horses. They needed the functional mexican or western saddle.

Two definite types of horses emerged among the riding horses of the United States — the Western horse and the English horse. The English horse is thought of as the Thoroughbred type — tall, long-legged, and graceful with long, ground covering strides. For a long time he remained mainly in the Eastern part of our country and was ridden with an English saddle. The Western horse was shorter, more heavily muscled, rugged, and a steady, hard worker. His short legs resulted in a short stride which was more comfortable to the man who rode all day than did the long stride of his Eastern counterpart. The cowboy chose his horse for comfort as well as 'savvy' or cow sense. Horses, then, are termed "English" or "Western" because of the type of tack used on them and because of their place of origin.

Although English Thoroughbreds were imported to the United States, there were quite a few breeds that originated here. Some were thought of as English horses and some as Western horses depending on what style of riding their promoters preferred. The Morgan is one of these breeds. Today he is ridden both English and Western. The American Saddle Horse, usually seen in the show ring under his own special style of English tack, is considered an English horse although

Two definite types emerged among the riding horses of the United States, the Western horse and the English horse. The English horse is tall, long-legged, and graceful with long, ground-covering strides. The Western horse is shorter, more heavily muscled, rugged and a steady hard worker in a variety of fields.

he has been used successfully as a cutting horse, which is a Western activity. He was originally developed because of his versatility. The Tennessee Walking Horse, again more familiar to us under English tack, is often ridden with a Western saddle. The American Quarter Horse and Appaloosa, usually thought of as Western horses, are both being ridden more and more under English tack. The type of saddle one uses on his horse is strictly a matter of personal taste until it comes to the world of the horse show. Here there are strict rules and traditions to follow. Those that fail to follow these are unsuccessful in competition. This book is confined to an explanation of the various 'seats' ridden with an English saddle, and the types of horses generally used with each. The appropriate clothing will also be discussed. ■

CHAPTER TWO

GOALS OF EQUITATION

Equitation is the art of horseback riding. Almost every horse show advertises equitation classes. These are classes where the rider only is judged. The horse, theoretically, is not supposed to count. It is true, however, that without a good mount, the equitation rider has difficulty competing successfully.

When one takes up horseback riding as a sport, he usually has little thought as to exactly what is involved. Perhaps he has seen others riding and decided it looked like fun. Perhaps he is an animal lover who has read horse stories and finally takes the opportunity to try it for himself. Usually he rents a horse or rides a friend's horse before he decides to purchase one of his own. He will very often take some riding lessons. In any case, the casual rider is not a student of equitation. To him, riding is an enjoyable pastime and nothing more. He is interested in the physical pleasure and mental stimulation involved but is not interested in the various theories developed over the centuries. This is not meant as a criticism because it is from this group of casual riders and horse enthusiasts that the true students of equitation evolve. Few begin with the idea of spending years studying equitation; pleasure is the immediate goal.

When one decides that he wants to really learn what horses and horseback riding are all about, he should choose a competent professional instructor to initiate his education. He cannot learn this from a book. He should attend as many clinics and horse activities as possible. He should expect to spend years learning to become an educated horseman; as in becoming a piano virtuoso, it does not happen overnight.

Why should equitation instruction be considered important even for the casual rider? In the first place, few would operate an automobile or an unfamiliar machine without some instruction. A horse, although not a dangerous animal, is an animal capable of his own thoughts which do not always coincide with those of his rider. He is a creature of habit and instinct. If the rider does not understand how the horse's mind works and what controls him, he can find himself in big trouble. All the tales of woe one hears from people who ride

Few horses are comfortable with beginners on them. Beginners pull on the horse's mouth for balance, bouncing around on their backs and screaming for no reason.

without benefit of prior instruction are unfortunate. But one can't help thinking he got only what could be expected for being so ill-advised as to get on a horse with such limited knowledge and absolutely no professional guidance. Even the most docile equine will take matters into his own hands when his unknowing rider annoys him and hinders his movements.

One of the primary goals of equitation, then, is the *safety* of the rider. The rider learns to ride correctly so that he is safe while riding. He learns how the horse thinks and how he responds to various aids and outside influences. He learns how to manage the horse so that his rides terminate as enjoyably as they began.

Another goal is the *comfort* of the horse and rider. Few beginners are comfortable on the horse. They have to develop the proper muscles and learn how to sit correctly in order to be physically comfortable. They have to also develop confidence and the proper attitude toward riding in order to be mentally comfortable.

Few horses are comfortable with beginners on them. Mentally, they become nervous and fearful because they cannot understand the attempts at control or the pain associated with the typical, unco-   **11**

A good seat may be defined as that exhibited by a rider having a great amount of security with the least amount of effort.

ordinated, uneducated commands of the neophyte. Beginners pull on the horse's mouth for balance, and bounce around on their backs and scream at the slightest cause. Watch a horse with a beginner on his back. His ears are half back and his whole expression is one of annoyance. The same horse ridden by a reasonably good rider will have an alert look without the unhappy expression. Few people really want to create discomfort for the horse yet, through ignorance, they continue to do so because they make no attempt to learn how to make the horse *comfortable*.

Developing a good seat and position is probably the goal most of us think of when we consider riding instruction. A good seat may be defined as that exhibited by a rider having a great amount of security with the least amount of effort. In other words, the rider has assumed a relaxed position that becomes as natural to him as walking down the street. Yet he is prepared at any moment, should the horse shy or bolt, to maintain his balance and security with *grip*. Leg grip should not be used unless necessary to stay atop the horse. A steady gripping will tire a rider's legs to the point where they quiver and become weak. A good position should be relaxed to absorb shocks. The

rider should not sit in the saddle as he would in an easy chair; he

A good equitation rider not only looks good on the horse, he also understands the horse and can obtain the most the horse is capable of at any given moment.

should sit lightly. He should be sensitive to his horse. The horse will "talk" to the rider by ear position, body movements and other actions if the rider will learn to "listen" to him. A good rider knows what the horse will do a second before he does it. A good rider has good balance so that he does not use the reins and horse's mouth to stay aboard. A rider rides by balance alone, but grip is used when necessary to preserve the balance.

If the rider has developed a good, secure, balanced position, he will no doubt have good hands. Good hands are independent hands; they do not follow the movements of the rider's body. They do not over-communicate to the horse. They do not annoy the horse. Once the rider has acquired good, light hands, he should work toward educating his hands. Educated hands are hands that are not only good, but are also those which know when to give and take. They can respond to the horse at the correct time. They know how to work with the horse to achieve the greatest results.

A good equitation rider not only looks good on the horse, he also understands the horse and can obtain the most the horse is capable of at any given moment. A good instructor teaches the student how to obtain the best results from each individual horse he rides. The more horses one has the opportunity to ride, the better rider he will become. ■

13

CHAPTER THREE

BASIC ENGLISH EQUITATION

All types of equitation, including Western, are basically the same. The good rider is a balanced rider. He is not only balanced in the saddle, he is in balance with his horse. A good saddle, English or Western, is designed so that the deepest part of the seat is over the horse's center of balance. This center of balance is located behind the withers — the exact location depends on what kind of horse it is, his conformation, and his training. The center of balance, or center of gravity as it is also termed, of the extremely collected American Saddle Horse will be farther back than that of the hunter type horse which has a lower, more natural head carriage. The center of balance will be more forward at the gallop than at the trot. The beginning rider should spend many hours riding without stirrups so that he learns to depend upon his balance to maintain his seat. Balance, of course, is preserved by the leg grip when necessary.

The rider sits in the deepest part of his saddle and positions his body squarely to the front. Any deviation in a square position will result in a lopsided moving horse. Remember that the horse is affected by the weight of the rider. Consider a 150 pound man carrying a 20 pound child piggy-back. He will be very aware of the movements of this child. The 1,000 pound horse carrying a 150 pound man is also very conscious of the movements of the rider on his back. If the rider develops the habit of always leaning to the right or left, the horse will have to use his body in an unbalanced way to compensate for this uneven distribution of weight. The results will be less than desirable.

The rider must always keep his head up and eyes forward or in the direction he is going. If he must look down to detect a canter lead or posting diagonal, he should drop his eyes instead of allowing the whole head to go forward. A rider's head is heavy and his constant looking down will pull his entire body more forward and round the shoulders. It is important for the rider to watch where he is going. The horse must be directed in his every step if he does not have a definite path to follow. The rider should be aware of this, especially during equitation figures so that he can guide the horse properly. If

The rider sits in the deepest part of the saddle and positions his body squarely to the front. Any deviation will result in a lopsided moving horse.

he neglects to guide the horse's every step, the course will be an uncertain one.

The rider's arms hang in a natural position at his sides. His hands are held in a straight line from the elbow down through the arm to the bit in the horse's mouth. The arms and the shoulders work as an extension of the rein; they work as if they were on springs ready to give or take. The rider uses his hands in an independent manner. If the rider's body is bouncing to the horse's trot, his hands must remain still. The rider learns to use them as aids completely detached from himself. The hands are the most important lines of communication between the rider and his horse. If the rider communicates unnecessarily or too frequently, the horse will tune out; communication will cease to be important to him. The rider, as a beginner, should ride with loose reins so that he does not needlessly annoy the horse. As he becomes a better, more balanced rider, he learns to ride more and more on (bit) contact so that he is able to influence his horse more subtly.

The rider's inner thighs are close to the saddle and his knee caps are pointed straight ahead. If the upper leg is in the proper position, the lower leg and foot are more apt to be in the proper position also. The rider's heels are lower than his toe and his feet are in a natural position as when walking — almost parallel to the horse's sides. The balls of the feet — which are the strongest part of the sole — rest on the tread of the stirrup iron. The stirrup irons should be wide enough so that the rider can move his feet freely in and out of them. This is a safety precaution. Often Hunt Seat riders push their feet "home" in the stirrups — pushed in to the heel. This helps them maintain their stirrups during the hunt.

The stirrup leather hangs perpendicular to the ground. The stirrup irons are the rider's floor. They must be directly under his body to be most effective. If the stirrup irons are carried directly under the rider's body, there will be a vertical line from the toe to the knee and the hip to the heel. The rider can test the correctness of his leg position by standing in the stirrups while balancing himself with his hands on the horse's neck. If he is able to maintain his balance in this position as long as he wants to, his feet are in the proper position.

The stirrup iron is for balance. The rider rests his foot on the tread; he does not actively push down on the tread except when posting or jumping. If he should push down constantly, his feet would soon be asleep.

The rider does not merely hang his feet in the stirrup irons. The heels are pushed down. This provides security should the horse stumble or fall forward. This also lengthens the calf muscles so their use is more effective. The legs must give the impression of strength and firmness.

The means by which the rider communicates to the horse is the language of the aids. Aids are natural — hands, legs, voice, weight — and artificial — crops, spurs, martingale, etc. The rider must learn to use his aids to the best advantage of both himself and his horse. He must learn what aids and combination of aids will bring about the desired responses.

The horse's "motor" is in his rear. He begins all his movements with his hind legs. In order to ask for a forward movement, the rider must ask the hind legs to move off. This is done with a squeeze of the calf behind the girth. At the same time the rider moves his hips forward in the saddle as if he were trying to push the saddle toward the withers. These two movements tell the horse forward. One always gives the horse the benefit of the doubt when applying aids. Never kick violently when asking for a forward movement. The calves are squeezed. If the horse does not respond, they are squeezed harder. If this is not effective, the heels are used. The rider's aids become progressively stronger until the horse does respond. A good rider knows that the horse has been trained by a system of reward and

If the stirrup irons are carried correctly under the rider's body, there will be a "vertical" line from the toe to the knee and from the hip to the heel.

punishment with emphasis on the rewards. The "punishment" is the use of the legs, hands, etc., while the reward is the cessation of the use of these aids. The good rider applies the aids until he feels the horse *begin* to respond, then he should release them. If the horse does not follow through with his response, the rider re-applies the aids. The responsive horse is the one trained to respond to aids that were increasingly more subtle while the unresponsive horse has been trained to respond to the harsh aids of an uneducated trainer.

The hands control the horse's forehand. They not only control direction, they control speed. The hands and legs are almost always used together but not simultaneously. The horse has a rather simple brain and can respond to only one aid at a time. To apply both rein and leg pressure at the same time will confuse him. The legs are applied a little before the hands in most cases.

The voice is important in schooling but is *never* used in the show ring. The voice is useful for communication because its tone will have a definite effect on the horse if he has learned the meanings.

Weight, as already mentioned, is very important to the horse. An even distribution of the rider's weight will keep the horse on a straight line and balanced. Weight is used for forward movement, to retard speed, and when turning. More about this later.

After the rider has mounted, and before moving forward, he should adjust himself in the saddle as previously described — facing squarely forward with the head up. The heels are down and the thighs and knees are in. The back is straight but not stiff; the shoulders are down and back. The reins of the single rein bridle, usually a snaffle, are held either under the little fingers or between the ring and little fingers. The rein goes up through the hand and over the index finger. The thumb is placed on top to hold the reins in place. The fingers remain flexible and relaxed in order to better communicate with the horse. The hands are turned in such a way that the thumbs point toward the ears of the horse; the right thumb points to the left ear and the left thumb points to the right ear. The wrists are relaxed and flexible. Beware of "broken" wrists — wrists that are stiff and flexed in. The hands must be sensitive and feeling so that they can communicate softly. A good exercise for stiff fingers and wrists is shaking them until they are limp. Hold the reins lightly as if they were thin threads that will break.

The rider's stirrups may be adjusted from the ground before mounting. This is done by measuring the leather along the underside of the arm. The stirrup iron should fit under the armpit with no slack.

18 They may also be adjusted from the saddle after mounting. This is

The hands are turned in such a way that thumbs point toward the ears of the horse, the right thumb toward the left ear, the left thumb toward the right.

The rider's stirrups may be adjusted from the ground before mounting. This is done by measuring the leather along the underside of the arm.

When adjusting the stirrups from the saddle, the foot should be left in the iron as a safety precaution, and because it is easier to do with the foot assisting.

often necessary for the short rider with a tall horse who may find mounting easier with a long stirrup. When adjusting the stirrups from the saddle, the foot should be left in the iron as a safety precaution and because it really is easier to adjust with the foot assisting. The rider should hold his reins in one hand. One should never lose contact with the reins. The stirrup may then be raised or lowered as necessary.

The correct adjustment of the stirrups will depend on what seat one is riding. The Balanced Seat rider will find that the stirrups adjusted to his ankle bone, measured when the feet are out of the stirrups and the rider is sitting in the deepest part of his saddle, is very comfortable for pleasure riding on the flat. The Forward, or Hunt Seat rider who plans to work over fences will adjust his stirrups to just above his ankle bone. The Saddle Seat rider will adjust his stirrups to below his ankle bone. Stirrups that are too short inhibit the rider's use of his legs and do not let him sit deep in his saddle. Stirrups that are too long create an insecure seat for the rider who is constantly losing them or reaching for them.

When the rider has decided his position is acceptable, he will *prepare* to ask the horse to walk forward. It is not fair to the horse to catch him by surprise with an application of the aids. He is not ready to listen and will not respond, or will respond in a startled manner.

The Balanced Seat rider will find that the stirrups adjusted even with his ankle bone is very comfortable for pleasure riding on the flat. The Hunt Seat rider will adjust them to just above the ankle bone, while the Saddle Seat rider will adjust the iron of the stirrups just below the ankle.

The rider prepares the horse for a command by shortening the reins and tightening the legs. Through his aids he says, "Listen to me!" The horse does listen and responds well to the rider's command — if the command is understood. The rider must learn the appropriate application of aids. He cannot expect the horse to try to interpret a series of jerks, thumps, and bounces to mean walk forward. Too many riders blame the horse for disobeying when the poor animal just couldn't understand what was expected of him. The rider must be very sure he is communicating correctly with the horse.

After the rider has prepared the horse for the command to walk forward, he squeezes the calves behind the girth to signal the horse to move on. As he squeezes his legs, he pushes his hips forward in the saddle. He also pushes his hands slightly forward to allow the horse to stretch his neck out for balance as he takes his first step forward. If the rider's hands do not follow this forward thrust of the horse's head and neck, the horse may bump into the bit.

The *walk* is a natural gait. A gait is the way a horse moves. A natural gait means the horse is born knowing how to do this. Every horse born knows how to walk if he has four good legs under him. The walk is a four beat gait — each foot is picked up and put down separately. The walk is also a vertical gait. It is the only gait without a period of suspension when all four feet are off the ground. The rider does not have to contend with the bouncing of the faster gaits. He learns to relax his seat and supple his loin so that he can feel the movement of the horse under him. He follows these movements with his body. The walk is the best gait for working on the basic position, halting, turning, etc. The horse is usually relaxed when he walks — if he is allowed plenty of exercise on his own while on pasture. The rider must not let the horse relax to the point of dogging along half asleep. He should keep the horse walking in a lively manner by squeezing and releasing his legs in an alternate rhythm as if he himself were walking — left, right, left, right, etc. At the same time he pushes with his seat. The rider can set the rhythm and speed of the walk this way.

The rider's position remains the same when the horse is walking. If he is riding on a loose rein his hands are still. If he is riding on contact — a light feel of the horse's mouth through the weight of the reins — his hands will have to move forward and back as the horse raises and lowers his head. The horse balances with his head and neck and must move them. The walk is the gait where this is the most obvious. If the rider is riding on contact and does not follow the movements of the horse's head and neck, he will have a fussy, uncomfortable horse that resents the restraint.

The walk is a natural gait. A gait is the way a horse moves. A natural gait means the horse is born knowing how to do this.

The rider usually spends 10 minutes or so warming the horse up at a walk before he goes on to the faster gaits. The horse has to 'wake up' physically and mentally before he is able to work well. While he is warming up the horse, the rider can work on circles, halts, and various other suppling exercises beneficial to the horse. When the rider is ready to trot, he again prepares the horse by shortening the reins and tightening the legs. The aids for trotting are the same as for asking the horse to walk. The horse should trot his first steps at the same speed and cadence that his rider intends for him to continue. He should not start out slowly and gradually build up speed or vice versa.

The trot is another natural gait. It is a diagonal gait — the horse's diagonal pair of legs, left hind and right front and right hind and left front, move forward and back together. There is a period of suspension when all the horse's feet are off the ground. The horse's spine drops and, if the rider is not relaxed and supple, he is left suspended as the saddle disappears out from under him. As a diagonal pair of legs strikes the ground, the horse's spine raises to meet the rider's seat coming down. There is a hearty thump to the seat of the rider and to the back of the horse. To avoid this, the rider must learn to supple his loin, knees, hips, and ankles so they may absorb the shocks of the trot. The biggest error the rider can make is trying to protect himself by putting weight in the stirrups. This will stiffen the shock absorbers and the rider will bounce worse than ever. The rider without stirrups at the trot, although initially having certain problems of balance, will not bounce out of the saddle even though he can feel the bounce through his seat and back. The bounce is always there; it is the manner in which the rider accommodates himself to it that is important.

The rider does all his schooling at the trot while he is in the sitting position. This is the position where he can use his aids to the best advantage. His early lessons at the trot should be spent sitting with and without stirrups until he is able to sit in a relaxed manner.

The rider does learn to post as a comfort to himself and to his horse while they are on the trail. This is also required in equitation classes in the show ring. *Posting* is the rising and sitting of the rider in rhythm to the horse's trot. One posts to either the left diagonal pair of legs or to the right diagonal pair. The rider, unless acrobatically inclined, is unable to see the hind legs of the horse when mounted, so they are disregarded when one refers to the posting diagonals. The rider is able to see the horse's shoulder so this is his guide. He does not lower his head to observe the shoulder but rather lowers his eyes. If he is rising as the left shoulder moves forward, he is posting on the left diagonal. If he is rising as the right shoulder moves forward, he is posting on the right diagonal. In the riding ring, or when circling, the rider posts to the outside diagonal — he rises as the shoulder closest to the outside of the circle or next to the fence (whichever the case may be) moves forward. In the ring, the rider will post on the left diagonal going clock-wise and on the right diagonal going counter-clockwise. He changes his diagonal as he changes direction. This is done by sitting through one beat of the trot.

The main reason for posting on the outside diagonal is that the horse will take a longer stride with his outside diagonal pair of legs around the curves of the ring or a circle and the rider's posting will look more graceful if he is posting on the outside diagonal. On the trail the rider has his choice of diagonals but should remember that it will rest both him and his horse to change diagonals occasionally because posting on the right diagonal will tire the left side of the horse (the side that bears the rider's weight as he sits), and vice versa. The rider should also remember that if he continually posts on the same diagonal, the horse will become unevenly muscled and the result will be a one-sided horse that has difficulty with his canter leads and turns.

When the rider rises during posting, he rises only as far out of the saddle as necessary to avoid the bounce. The less he rises, the better

he will look, and the more secure will be his seat. The horse with the

As the rider sits down while posting, he lowers himself into the saddle by rolling back on his thighs; he does not go plop!

long stride will cause the rider to rise farther out of the saddle than the horse with the short stride. As the rider rises out of the saddle he will lean a little more forward than at the walk or sitting trot. Try getting out of a chair without leaning slightly forward — awkward to say the least. The rider uses his knees as a pivot point and the lower leg remains stationary. If the rider's stirrups are directly under his body, he will have little trouble in rising. As the rider sits down, he lowers himself into the saddle by rolling back on his thighs; he does not go plop! He never actually sits deep in the saddle when he is posting! rather he comes in contact with it just long enough to rise again. One of the best exercises is posting without stirrups. While this is initially quite tiring, it is a great muscle developer and the rider will be able to post more gracefully when he re-acquires his stirrups. This exercise is a favorite of the equitation judges.

The canter is a three beat natural gait with a period of suspension as the horse leaps forward. This is the gait where the various seats differ the most. The Forward, or Hunt Seat rider will lean markedly forward to be over the horse's center of gravity! The Saddle Seat rider will sit erect on his more collected horse! The Balanced Seat rider will sit just a little more forward than he would while at the trot, but this depends upon his horse. If the horse is a natural moving horse, the rider will be more forward than he would be while working his horse at a more collected canter — wherein he will be in a more vertical position.

When the horse canters, one lateral pair of legs go farther forward than the other lateral pair. These are the leading legs. In the ring, or in a circle, the horse must lead with the pair of legs to the inside of the ring, or he will have difficulty maneuvering the turns. If he is not on the inside lead (in order to maintain his balance) he may come to a trot, he may change leads, or he may continue on his unbalanced way. The rider, on foot, can pretend he is a horse and gallop around in circles. He will discover that when going to the right his right leg must 'lead' his left and vice versa or he feels awkward and unbalanced. Watch a child playing "horse," or watch a horse in pasture — they will naturally canter on the appropriate lead, changing leads as they change directions.

The horse's lead problems begin with his rider. He has learned to depend on his rider for commands. On his own, he knows what lead to take by the direction he, himself, plans to go. Under the influence of a rider he has no idea of the direction they will take. He learns to depend on his rider to tell him what canter leads to take. If the rider fails to apply the aids properly, the horse does the best he can and canters on the lead he thinks was asked for. If he is wrong in his guess, he is usually yanked down and swatted around a little, much to his chagrin and confusion. Few young horses in training, if signaled properly, fail to take the proper lead. The rider is the one who confuses the horse. The rider who says, "He won't take the right lead," would be better off saying, "I cannot signal this horse properly for the right lead."

An old horse with lead problems is usually not to be blamed, rather his previous riders. This does not apply to the horse with a temporary injury that refuses a particular lead to protect himself. The sensitive rider, tuned into his horse, will look for something amiss when all of a sudden his horse will not canter on a certain lead. There are some unsoundnesses that do not cause obvious lameness in their initial stages and show up only when it is almost too late to do anything about them.

When asking the horse to canter — and this is done by asking for a specific lead — the rider must realize that the horse asked to canter when turning to the left will naturally assume the left lead. The rider may apply *diagonal aids* to ask for the canter. The right leg behind the girth signals the horse's right hind leg to strike off, the left leg closes at the girth. The left rein, slightly tightened, will bend the horse in the direction of the left lead the horse is being asked to take. This is called a diagonal aid because of the diagonal line made by the rider's leg and hand aids. The rider pushes his hips forward as he uses his leg aids; he does not throw his entire weight forward by leaning forward over the horse's shoulder. This merely displaces his weight and does not influence the horse. Many horses will canter at a shift of the hips that will not canter as the rider leans forward. This leaning forward also puts the rider in a precarious position if the horse should change his first stride of the canter into a playful buck. As the horse strikes off into the canter the rider glances down to the shoulders to check the canter lead. The leading shoulder moves out ahead of the other. If the horse has incorrectly picked up the wrong lead, the rider should bring him quietly to a walk and ask again. The preparation for the canter, getting the horse's attention, is just as important as the actual aids for the canter. If the horse is not prepared for the command, his response will be less than perfect.

Another, and more popular, method of asking for the canter is the use of the *lateral aids*. These are so called because the rider will tighten the right rein and use the right leg behind the girth to ask for the left lead! these aids form a lateral line. The left leg is used at the girth to assist the right leg in asking for the canter. The idea of using lateral aids is to free the horse's leading shoulder to make it easier for him to strike off on that lead. The Saddle Seat rider always uses this method of asking for the canter. The Balanced Seat riders and Forward Seat riders can use either. Both methods are effective and acceptable! it just depends on personal preference — the way one's horse has been trained, or the preference of one's instructor.

The canter is a rocking gait; it is difficult for the beginner to sit. The rider must learn to sit deep in the saddle and to make certain that his seat *stays* deep in the saddle. It is all too easy for the rider to put too much weight in his stirrups and leave the saddle with each stride. This is not comfortable to either horse or rider. The rider should relax his hips and loin so that his spine at the waist works like a hinge. The upper body rocks back and forth with the motion of the horse, while the seat remains firmly in the saddle. The feet are balanced in the stirrups with no more weight in them than necessary to keep them from coming out of the irons. Some horses are more difficult to sit than others, but if the rider will practice without stirrups he will develop the feel and rhythm enabling him to be with his horse during the canter.

On the trail, the rider may· ask for whatever lead he wants the horse to take. In the ring the horse must always canter on the inside lead — the lead to the center of the ring. The only exception is during the counter-canter which is an exercise of more advanced equitation.

The rider must remember to canter an equal amount of the time on both leads so that the horse's musculature is evenly developed. Horse's are right or left handed the same as their riders.

The rider must not only understand the proper aids by which to communicate with the horse, he must also understand how to discipline the horse. The beginner must not feel threatened by the horse. The horse is timid and the few aggressive ones are easily bullied if the rider is so inclined. The rider will learn to achieve his goals through persistence and patience. When the horse responds properly, a pat and kind word will reinforce this response. If the horse fails to respond properly, analyze the reason and try again. The competent, experienced rider knows how to punish effectively without hurting the horse; the novice does not. His punishment can turn into abuse. Patience will work wonders with even the most stubborn animal if the rider does not lose his temper.

This brings to mind a particular case of a balker that would stop and not move unless he had his own way. His clever rider would pull a pocket edition of a novel from her pocket and read it until the horse decided to move again. The horse had learned he would be led to the barn when he balked. His new owner did not beat him up or use methods of less sensitive trainers; rather she let the horse think moving on was his own idea. Since it no longer got him to the barn, he gave up his notion. I have seen balkers brutally abused that never gave up the habit — rather they persisted in their stubbornness.

If the horse is being particularly disobedient, a firm thwack of a crop should straighten him out. The noise is more effective than the pain. The rider should never jerk the horse's mouth or hit him around the head. He will only damage the mouth and make the horse head-shy. The rider must be ready to enforce his commands as long as the commands are the proper ones. If the horse is continually allowed to be disobedient or to evade the rider's commands, he will quickly become spoiled. The rider must insist the horse carry through a given command if only for the sake of discipline. This is assuming that there is no physical reason for disobedience and that the horse does understand the command. The rider must actually ride his horse at all times and not be a mere passenger who lets the horse take what direction at what speed he prefers. The rider must always be in command even when the ride is a short, quiet walk through
the woods. ■

CHAPTER FOUR

THE SEATS OF THE ENGLISH RIDER

The Balanced Seat

At the end of the 19th century the Italian horseman, de la Gueriniere introduced the Balanced Seat. It was a modification of the Italian Forward Seat designed by Frederico Caprilli. It became the exclusive seat of the American Cavalry because they believed it to be a correct seat from both a mathematical and mechanical standpoint. It gives the greatest comfort to the horse with the least amount of effort to the rider. It may be adapted to any type of work. It is a very flexible seat and the rider can use any length of stirrup he prefers, depending on what he is doing.

As was mentioned previously, all seats depend on balance with grip preserving the balance when needed. The difference is in the techniques for maintaining balance. In the Balanced Seat the rider sits down in the saddle and is more vertical in position during the sitting trot and canter than the rider of the Forward Seat.

The horse of the Balanced Seat rider is trained to work in both a collected and extended manner. The rider adjusts his balance to compensate for this. If the horse is working in a natural manner, the rider will lean a little more forward at the trot and canter. His horse's balance is more forward because his head and neck are extended. If the horse is working at the collected gaits, his center of gravity is in the middle of his body and the rider assumes a vertical position. A Balanced Seat rider is able to adapt himself to whatever type of horse he is riding. This makes both horse and rider comfortable.

The Balanced Seat rider has his choice of saddles. Because there is no actual American Horse Shows Association class for the Balanced Seat Rider, his clothing and tack have never been officially defined as has the clothing and tack of the riders of other seats. However, the Balanced Seat rider is more apt to ride hunters and jumpers or dressage horses than he is the American Saddle Horse so will usually prefer a forward seat (jumping) or dressage saddle. Many riders who do quite a bit of hunting and jumping ride the Balanced Seat on the flat and assume the forward position over fences; many never jump but prefer pleasure riding.

The Balanced Seat rider is usually attired in clothing designed for the hunt field. Breeches, usually canary or rust, are worn if the rider plans to wear hunt boots. Hunt boots are high boots that fit snugly at the calf. They come as high as possible on the leg without interfering with the bend of the knee. If the rider prefers the English style jodhpurs for pleasure riding, they are acceptable, but low jodhpur boots are worn with these. This later combination is not usually seen in the show ring. The rider wears a wool or linen hunt coat, depending on the season. An equitation rider should wear a solid, dark color. A velvet hunt cap that matches the outfit is worn as protective head gear. The rider wears a choker or ratcatcher shirt with its own tie for informal wear. A stock tie is worn with more formal attire. Women should confine their hair in a net. Colored scarves should not be worn as they detract from the workmanlike appearance. Gloves complete the outfit.

The Balanced Seat rider has his choice of bridles. The most preferred is the snaffle bridle. The reins should be plaited or laced. The bit should be of good quality and should be the egg butt type. This type is constructed so that the rings do not pinch the corners of the horse's mouth. The mouthpiece should be thick; the thicker it is, the milder. The bit should fit the horse's mouth; neither too wide so as to slide annoyingly around, nor too narrow to pinch. The bridle should be adjusted so that the bit fits snugly into the corners of the mouth. The new bridle should be thoroughly oiled so it will be protected from sweat, etc. Oiling will preserve the life of the leather and prevent its cracking. The bit should be rinsed off each time it is taken out of the horse's mouth and the leather soaped if possible.

A leather girth is usually used by the Balanced Seat rider. These are strong girths but must be kept clean or the horse may develop girth sores. A string girth is excellent for the times of the year when the horse is apt to be splashing through the mud, because it can be tossed into the washing machine. It is also very good for preventing girth sores. Some girths have elastic ends which make a very comfortable arrangement for the horse.

A saddle pad is used to protect the horse from the saddle, and the saddle from the horse. The more washable these are, the better.

The Hunt Seat
Although one hears the term *Hunt Seat* frequently, it has never been properly defined. The American Horse Shows Association Rule Book does not really define it for the riders competing in what is

A Balanced Seat rider is usually attired in clothing designed for the hunt field. Breeches, either canary or rust, are worn if the rider plans to wear hunt boots.

termed Hunt Seat Equitation. Usually the riders in these classes are riding the Forward Seat, often called the Hunt Seat; the Balanced Seat or the Dressage Seat. A great variety of positions are found in the hunt field. The old Hunt Seat was a ghastly sight to behold. The rider, over fences, leaned back as far as possible with his feet "on the dashboard." How he and his horse survived, heaven only knows. Eventually, because of the Italian, Frederico Caprilli, a more practical seat for the hunt field was developed. This is now known as the Forward Seat.

The Forward Seat

This seat was conceived to unite the rider with a forward moving horse. Basically, the rider places his weight so that the horse can carry it in the easiest possible manner. The rider sits on his crotch and pelvic bones. He balances in his stirrup irons to keep in balance over the horse's withers. As the horse increases his speed, his neck and head move farther forward. This shifts his entire weight farther forward. The rider, in turn, moves his weight and balance farther forward by rolling more forward on the thighs and putting more weight in the stirrups. He does this in order to be over the horse's center of gravity. This seat theoretically allows full freedom of natu- **31** ral movements to the horse. The rider's position is such that he can guide and control his mount without limiting his freedom. The proponents of the Forward Seat maintain that a beginner naturally assumes this position and is better able to control his horse. Ted Sloan, the American jockey, first introduced this seat in this country. When he began winning, other jockeys adopted it and still use it today. Of course, they shortened their stirrups and the seat evolved to meet the more extreme needs of a jockey.

The hands are held several inches in front of the pommel and are separated by the width of the horse's shoulders. There is a straight line from the elbow to the bit. The rider maintains light contact without inhibiting the horse's freedom.

This is the seat for the rider who enjoys hunting and jumping, although it is often considered extreme for riding on the flat. Many Balanced Seat riders adopt this seat over fences as was previously mentioned, yet resume their Balanced Seat for riding on the flat.

When the rider jumps, he places his weight in the stirrups and rolls forward out of the saddle as the horse goes over the obstacle.

The type of saddle used is the forward seat, or jumping saddle that was originally an Italian design. The seat of the saddle is deep to offer maximum security to the rider. For further security there are knee rolls under the flaps. Quite often there are calf rolls. These saddles are very comfortable and good for pleasure riding. They are made by most saddle makers, and come in various price ranges depending on the quality of leather used, the country where they were made, and how well they are built. The buyer must remember that he gets what he pays for and although a less expensive saddle may look good, they do not always wear well. A well constructed saddle is made on a spring tree so as to fit most horses.

The types of bridles for the Forward Seat rider are the snaffle, as previously described, the Pelham, and the Weymouth. The Pelham bridle is a bit with two pairs of rings on the shanks. To these are attached two pairs of reins. The top pair of reins is called the snaffle reins. Their use is very mild — milder than a snaffle bit because there is no nutcracker action. The lower pair of reins are the curb reins. These work in a lever action on the poll, and on the bars of the mouth, as does a regular curb bit. These two pair of reins are used independently; they may also be used together. Their effect is usually milder than the use of the Weymouth bridle but not as mild as the snaffle. The Weymouth bridle will be described in the section on Saddle Seat equitation.

The rider's clothing for the Forward Seat is the same as that of

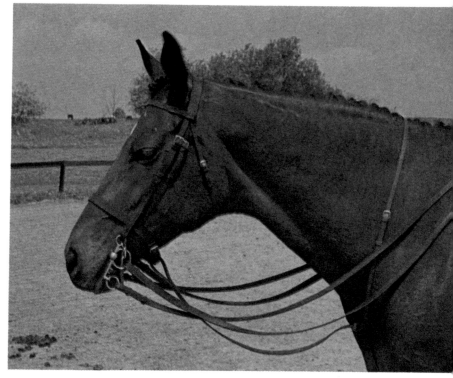

The Pelham bridle is a bit with two pairs of rings on the shanks. To these are attached two pairs of reins, referred to as the snaffle and the curb.

the Balanced Seat rider. The member of a hunt wears what that particular hunt dictates.

The type of horse ridden by the Hunt Seat rider, and Balanced Seat rider as well, is a Thoroughbred type horse. It is a tall horse, (a taller horse doesn't have to jump as high as his shorter brother) with good substance. The horse can be of any breed or mixture of breeds but he should look refined and display good breeding. He should move with long, low strides so as to maximize the use of his energy. This is opposed to the horse with high action that wastes his energy in raising his legs instead of covering the ground. The horse should have a good mouth and be willing to move forward. He should have a long, graceful neck so that he is light on the forehand. The heavy, short-necked horse has a tendency to be heavy on the forehand. He should be athletically inclined.

The Dressage Seat

Dressage is just beginning to achieve popularity in this country. It is perhaps the most misunderstood seat of them all. In the first place, dressage is the French word for training. Dressage is a system of schooling the horse and perfecting his natural movements so that he is obedient and a pleasure to ride. It is a series of gymnastic exercises to create a supple, well-balanced, athletic horse. It is a method of training that creates a very obedient horse presenting the appearance of elegance with a maximum amount of ease.

Most horsemen are familiar with the classical dressage of the Spanish Riding School of Austria. Few of us are accomplished enough to train our horses to perform these remarkable feats, all natural to the free horse. Few horses are naturally athletic enough to go on to be trained in these advanced movements of dressage just as few of the human race are capable of becoming advanced in their chosen fields of sporting events — it takes a special horse, or a special person. This does not mean that we should not even attempt the lower levels of dressage training. Even if we accomplish just a few of the exercises or movements, our horses will become the better for it, and so will we.

Dressage is *not* trick riding. Circus riding is trick riding and cannot be called dressage. This is one area of misunderstanding. Few horsemen want a trick horse in their barn.

The dressage horse moves with his center of balance in the middle of his back. The rider balances on the horse by sitting squarely in the saddle — usually a deep seated saddle with long straight flaps known as a dressage saddle. The rider's stirrups are long so that he can use his legs most effectively. He rides on his toes more than any other rider except the Saddle Seat rider. The German school emphasizes a supple loin to maintain contact with the horse and influence his movements.

The dressage rider schools his horse with a snaffle bridle and uses the Weymouth only for more advanced work. The Weymouth of the dressage rider is not the same as that of the Saddle Seat rider. The dressage Weymouth has thick, mild bits, thicker cheeks, and plain browband.

The dressage rider wears the clothes described for the Forward Seat rider. He may, however, wear white breeches for showing at lower levels. As he progresses to higher levels, he is required to wear more formal attire consisting of white breeches and a shad belly coat. A high silk hat takes the place of the hunt cap in the higher levels. The dressage classes are individual events. Each movement of the test is scored from 0 to 10. The judge writes comments so the rider

Dressage is a series of gymnastic exercises designed to create a supple, well-balanced, athletic horse. It is a method of training that creates a very obedient horse presenting the appearance of elegance with the maximum amount of ease. While the advanced movements are for special individuals, the lower levels are for all horses.

can improve himself and his horse. Dressage requires a great deal of self-discipline, but it is extremely rewarding. The dressage-trained horse, whether used in the hunt field, the show ring, or the rodeo arena, is such a pleasure to ride because he is trained to be an athlete. He is maneuverable and obedient. It is the difference between driving a truck and a car with power steering.

The Saddle Seat

The Saddle Seat is the most recent variation of the seats. It was designed for maximum efficiency when showing the American Saddle Horse. This type of horse is trained to perform with high leg action in an extremely collected way. The rider uses a very flat English saddle called the cut-back saddle. This is a very flat saddle with four inches cut out of the pommel so it will fit down on the horse's back yet leave a place for his withers. It is a very long saddle so the rider can sit further back on the horse — the American Saddle Horse's center of balance (when showing) is designed to be further back than that of any other breed of horse. The flaps are cut back slightly to give greater freedom to the horse's shoulders. The design of the saddle makes the horse look shorter backed and longer necked.

The rider is at a vertical position at a standstill but leans more

The Saddle Seat rider is at a vertical position at a standstill, but leans more forward so as not to get behind the horse at the trot and canter.

forward so as not to get behind the horse at the trot and canter. His stirrups are longer than those of the riders of the other seats — below the ankle bone. They should not, however, be so long for the equitation rider that posting looks like an effort. The equitation *rider* certainly displays what looks like a more comfortable seat than the professional *trainer*. The Saddle Seat rider rides by balance more than any other rider. Riders of Morgans, Tennessee Walking Horses, and Arabians have adopted this saddle and a modified Saddle Seat for their own show ring use, but it truly belongs to the American Saddle Horse people. Occasionally one sees an Appaloosa, Paint, or Quarter Horse in Saddle Horse attire. However, it usually looks out of place because these breeds are trained to move in a more natural way than the collected, lofty way-of-going of the American Saddle Horse. The Quar-

ter Horse is much more at home in Hunt Seat attire, as are most

Paints and Appaloosas.

The Weymouth (also called the full bridle or double bridle) is a must for the Saddle Seat rider. This is a bridle with a combination of a thin wire snaffle bit called a bradoon plus a curb bit, usually long shanked. This can be a very severe combination if incorrectly used, but in the hands of a sympathetic rider, a great deal of style and brilliance can be created through their use. Unfortunately, too many horses ridden exclusively in these bits end up with very insensitive mouths. The leather cheekpieces of these show bridles are very thin and elegant; the browband is very decorative.

The American Saddle Horse is trained to work off the snaffle bit for control of direction and speed; the curb bit is for collection. To hold two pair of reins, the rider brings the snaffle rein under his little finger. The curb rein goes between the snaffle rein and the horse's neck — it is the inside rein. It passes between the middle and ring fingers or the ring and little fingers. The two reins then pass over the index finger and the thumb holds them in place. The rider's hands and arms are held in a position approximately parallel to the ground or at belt buckle level. The horse has a naturally high head carriage and thus the hands are carried high to maintain the straight line from elbow to bit.

Because the rider uses an extremely long stirrup he usually carries a whip as an aid. The legs (although not theoretically so) are not used in the saddle seat as much as in any other seat. The legs from the knees are pushed away from the horse's barrel. They are too far away to come into contact when necessary, thus the whip.

The Saddle Seat, too extreme for the pleasure rider, is reserved for the show ring and the three and five-gaited American Saddle Horse.

The Saddle Seat rider wears a suit consisting of Kentucky jodhpurs and a matching saddle coat. This coat is longer than the hunt coat. The rider may wear formal attire in the evening classes. The hard derby is the acceptable head wear and low jodhpur boots are worn on the feet. The rider may wear a vest. He should wear gloves, as should all English riders. Dark, conservative colors are preferred. The rider's hair is confined in a net. A colorful flower may be worn in the lapel.

The Park Saddle

There is another type English saddle available. This is called the park saddle. It's a flat saddle with straight flaps. It is used mostly for pleasure riding. Most English riders are specializing in one particular seat so the park saddle is enjoying less popularity than it once did. ■

CHAPTER FIVE

EQUITATION EXERCISES

The Figure Eights
This pattern is made up of two circles joined in the center. They should be the same size and shape and they must be *circles,* not two diagonal lines with a curve at each end.

The rider learns the figure at the walk, progresses to the trot and later to the canter.

The rider picks a center point and rides to this. He halts to allow the judge, if he is in the show ring, to begin observing the figure. The rider executes a circle to the left or right, whichever he desires, then returns to his starting point. Throughout the circle, his horse's body has maintained a continuous curve following the arc of the circle. As the rider approaches the center of the "eight," he straightens his horse's body for a stride or two, then begins his second circle. The rider returns to his starting point and halts for a few seconds to indicate the completion of the figure. The importance of the rider's control of speed and direction cannot be over-emphasized.

At the posting trot, the rider will continuously post on the diagonal to the outside of the circles he is describing. He will change his diagonal in the center as he changes directions.

At the canter, the rider will change leads as he changes directions. He must be on the inside lead for each circle. The Saddle Seat rider will halt to change his leads. The Hunt Seat rider will return to a walk.

The Serpentine
This is a series of half circles down an imaginary center line. The rider demonstrates his ability to control the direction and speed of his horse as well as his own ability to change diagonals at a posting trot and leads at a canter as necessary. The rider changes leads or diagonals as he crosses the imaginary center line after completing one half circle and before he begins his next half circle.

The Turn On The Forehand
The exercise *turn on the forehand* teaches the horse to move away from the rider's legs. It teaches the rider to use his legs properly when controlling the direction of the hindquarters. It is helpful when opening

The turn on the forehand is an exercise that teaches the horse to move away from the rider's legs. It is helpful when opening gates.

gates.

The rider halts the horse about a yard from the rail. He wants to change directions by asking the horse to move his haunches around his forehand. The rider tightens his outside rein slightly and uses his outside leg behind the girth. He pushes the horse's haunches away from the rail. As the horse takes a step, the rider relaxes his leg pressure. Again he applies pressure for another step and so on until the horse is facing the other direction. The horse should not back up, but he will if the reins are too tight. He will walk forward if they are too loose. The rider must find the happy medium. The rider's inside leg will close at the girth to maintain impulsion — so the horse knows he is to continue movement. As the horse completes the turn, he should be asked to move forward. Once the horse and rider have mastered this turn in both directions, they can practice away from the rail and increase the turn to 360 degrees.

The Turn On The Haunches

This is easier for the horse to do than the turn on the forehand, but it is not as easy for the rider to apply the aids. The turn on the haunches is changing directions by moving the front feet around the hind feet, **39**

The horse should back promptly and with a diagonal leg movement.

Riding without stirrups helps the rider develop good balance.

the inside hind foot being the pivot point. The hind feet move up and down but should not move forward or back.

The rider halts along the rail and brings both hands to the inside of the ring and slightly back. The outside leg moves back to act as a holding leg. The inside leg is used at the girth to maintain impulsion. The horse should take each step deliberately when asked.

Backing The Horse

The horse should back promptly and with a diagonal leg movement. The rider halts the horse. He applies his legs as if asking the horse to walk on, then retards the forward movement with rein pressure. The horse should take a step back. He is asked for each step he takes by a giving and taking with the reins and a squeezing and releasing of leg pressure. The rider should not cluck. The horse should back indefinitely but only three steps are required in the show ring. He should be walked, trotted, or cantered promptly forward. The horse should not toss his head or show other signs of resistance. If the horse refuses to back, someone on the ground should push him back and he should be praised for each step he takes. Backing is difficult for a horse and even more so with a rider on him.

Riding Without Reins And Stirrups

One of the most beneficial exercises for the improvement of the rider's balance is riding at all three gaits without reins. Obviously the horse will have to be quiet and willing to work without continual guidance from his rider. The rider will work in a small enclosed area so that any necessary control will be kept to a minimum.

The rider should hold the reins at the buckle or stitched area. He should not drop them on the horse's neck because the horse could toss his head and flip the reins over his head to the ground. The rider may work with his arms crossed in front of his chest, with hands on hips, with hands on knees, or wherever he wishes. The important point is learning to use the body for balance and not the hands clutched to the reins, and thus the horse's mouth.

Riding without stirrups has already been mentioned so this point will be passed over lightly. The rider, when he feels a bit secure, can work without reins and stirrups at all three gaits. If he has the opportunity to have someone lunge his horse with him on his back, he will quickly develop good balance. The horse should be trained to work quietly on the lunge line and respond to vocal commands. The rider, of course, can assist in the horse's control on the lunge line, but the quieter the horse works in both directions, the more beneficial this exercise will be to the rider. ■

CHAPTER SIX

RIDING OVER FENCES

Once the rider has advanced to the point of being a successful rider at all three gaits and can execute the equitation tests of the American Horse Shows Association (address: 527 Madison Avenue, New York, New York 10022), he might consider learning to jump if he is so inclined. Many equitation schools will begin jumping exercises with the advanced beginners and low intermediate riders, but these riders do not go on with their jumping until much later unless they are quite talented initially. Jumping requires a great deal of balance and control of the various parts of the body. It requires the ability to pace the horse and anticipate his movements — over the fence or around it? It requires the good seat and hands that are developed slowly with a good deal of hard work on the student's part.

Training the rider to jump is quite like training the horse except that the student of jumping rides a very cadenced, steady, thoroughly trained hunter that seldom refuses or runs out. The rider learns to handle himself over the fence before he learns to handle the horse over the fence.

Initially the rider will practice the forward, or galloping position. Once he can maintain this position at a walk, trot, and canter without losing his balance, he is ready for jumping. Meanwhile he can work over low cavalettis to learn to guide the horse to the center of the obstacle.

The forward position enables the horse to jump freely without interference from the rider. It enables the rider to stay with his horse over the fence.

To move into the forward position, the rider tightens his knees and thighs and strengthens his leg position. He rolls forward on his thighs until he is out of the saddle. His heels are down. His shoulders are back and his eyes straight ahead. His hands are along the side of the horse's neck maintaining a straight line from elbow to bit. He maintains this position, catching himself with his hands if he should start to fall back, until he decides to sit down again.

Logs, four by fours, or something similar are placed on the ground five to six feet apart. The rider trots the horse over these, maintaining

To move into the forward position, the rider tightens his knees and thighs, while he rolls forward until his seat is out of the saddle.

a forward position. The horse must be guided to the center of these obstacles and not be allowed to speed up or slow down. It is important to maintain impulsion or the horse may clumsily stumble over the obstacles instead of neatly trotting through them without a touch. Once the rider has mastered these, a pole may be placed on two cement blocks. The rider will trot over this, going into a forward position about a stride before the obstacle and remaining there for a stride or two after. The horse will not jump this but rather trot over it in stride. The rider can space these obstacles around the ring and down through the center so that he may learn to guide the horse over a course of obstacles. The rider can also canter over these. It is important not to jerk the horse's mouth but rather follow with the hands as the horse goes over the obstacle. If the rider has a tendency to fall back or be left behind the horse over the fences, he could close his hands on the

The rider trots the horse over logs, four by fours or something similar placed on the ground five to six feet apart. This teaches coordination and timing.

It is important not to jerk the horse's mouth, but rather follow with the hands as the horse goes over the obstacle.

horse's neck for support or grab a handful of mane until he has attained some semblance of balance. This is not the greatest habit to get into but it is better than spoiling a good horse by punishing his mouth each time he jumps. Once balance is acquired, the rider can work to improve his hand position.

If the rider approaches the jump at a trot, he should sit the trot. This will help him go into the forward position when he is ready to and he will be less confused than if he is trying to work the forward position in somewhere in the posting sequence.

The rider should not learn to jump by himself because he will not be aware of his mistakes. He should seek professional help rather than the help of an acquaintance who just happens to have a horse that jumps. ■

SECTION TWO

THE TRAINING OF THE ENGLISH HORSE

CHAPTER SEVEN

BASIC TRAINING

We will assume that the young horse is a two year old. He has been halter broken, will tolerate grooming and clipping, allows his feet to be handled. Hopefully the owner has not over-handled the colt to the point where he has lost respect for people.

The horse should be bridled and saddled each day until he shows acceptance of this equipment. A thick-mouthed snaffle bit is the most comfortable. It is a help to leave a reinless bridle on the colt for several hours each day, including throughout a feeding. He will have plenty of time to chew the bit and to try to spit it out. Once he has accepted it and holds it quietly in his mouth, the trainer knows his purpose has been accomplished. The saddle should be placed carefully on the colt's back and the girth easily tightened just enough to keep the saddle from turning. An English saddle is light and is the least cumbersome to use. The stirrup leathers should be removed so they will not frighten the colt or catch something in the stall. The saddle should be left on the colt for an hour or two at a time.

This process should be carried out for a week or two until the colt has accepted the entire tacking up process with no squirming or rolling of eyes.

The next step is to teach the colt to work on the lunge line. This is excellent ground work for preparing the colt for mounted work. Not only does it supple him, it increases his muscle tone, develops his balance, and teaches him to respond to voice commands.

Two people are usually needed at first — one with the lunge line and whip and the other leading the colt in a circle until he gets the idea of staying out on the end of the lunge line. The colt is worked an even amount of time in both directions. The first lesson should include halting, using the word "Whoa," as well as walking on the command "Walk." The colt will have a short attention span and be easily distracted. Two short lessons of 10 to 15 minutes apiece at first will be better than one 20 minute lesson.

As soon as the colt responds to the commands "Walk" and "Whoa" and will work in both directions without assistance, the trainer can ask for the trot. He uses the sharp command "Trot" and flicks the colt on the tail with the whip. This will not hurt the colt, but will

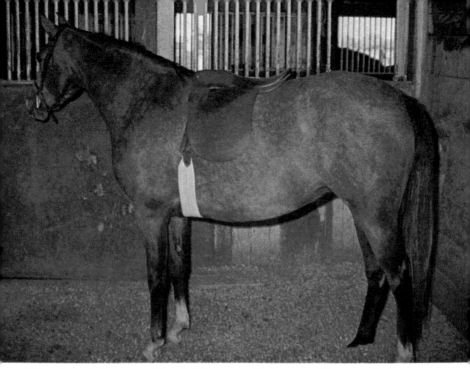

It is a help to leave a reinless bridle on a colt for several hours each day, including throughout a feeding. He will soon accept it and hold it in his mouth quietly.

send him forward. The trainer should keep the colt in the trot until he gives the command "Walk." Each time the colt attempts to return to the walk on his own, the trainer repeats the command "Trot" and flicks the colt on the tail with the whip. The colt should be brought from a trot to a walk to a halt. Do not expect him to halt from a trot.

The colt is lunged with his saddle and bridle on. The reins may be removed or fastened to the saddle so they do not tangle in the colt's legs. The lunge line is passed through the ring of the snaffle bit, over the top of the colt's head, and snaps to the snaffle ring on the other side. This is changed as the horse's direction is changed. The trainer has the most control and can keep the horse's bend toward the inside of the circle. One of the important goals of lunging the horse is to teach him to bend his body in the arc of the circle he is describing. Side reins may be used but should not be tight. An overcheck is helpful because the colt will be unable to stop to eat.

The colt can be taught to canter on the lunge line when he understands the commands of whoa, walk, and trot. It is more difficult for the colt to canter on the lunge line because the circle is small and he has

The colt is lunged with his saddle and bridle on. The reins may be removed or fastened to the saddle so they do not tangle in the colt's legs.

to learn to balance around this continuous curve. The trainer will have to be persistent in helping the colt maintain the canter without frightening him to the point where he is running because of fear. It is easier for the colt to go into the canter from the trot so the trainer should keep this in mind. When he wants to halt the colt, it is important at first to bring him to the halt progressively through the trot and walk.

Throughout this entire process of working with the colt — saddling, bridling, teaching him to work at all three gaits on the lunge line — the trainer can occasionally lean over the colt's back asking him to bear more and more weight. The colt, by the time he is actually mounted, will think nothing of the rider on his back.

The trainer will need a trustworthy assistant either to mount the colt for the first few times or to keep hold of the lunge line while the trainer mounts. The colt should not be allowed complete freedom when first mounted because he will not understand what is going on. He may become frightened.

To break up the routine of lunging the colt, the trainer should line drive the colt each day. This is an important step preceding mounting because it teaches the colt to respond to the bit. The stirrups will

Line driving is an important step preceding mounting, because it teaches the colt to respond to the bit. Tie the stirrups under the animal's stomach.

have to be replaced and adjusted so that the reins pass through them to the driver's hands without a bend in the reins. The stirrups should be tied down under the colt's stomach so that they do not swing around and frighten him. The driver will work the colt at a walk and trot asking for circles and various large turns as well as halting. He should use his voice with the same tone as when lunging. It is the tone that the colt learns rather than the words. When the colt is responsive to the reins and voice when lunging and line driving, the trainer can prepare for mounting.

The rider should receive a leg up because this is less frightening to the colt than mounting with the stirrup. The colt should be led at a walk and when he shows signs of relaxing, the trainer can begin with a minimum amount of rein control while his assistant moves further out on the lunge line. An enclosed riding ring is the best place to start riding the colt. He will realize he is confined and will pay more attention to the work at hand. All aids should be gentle but exaggerated. The colt will not understand the leg aids and may resent them; he will certainly not respond to them. As the rider asks for a walk, he uses his voice to give the command. He squeezes his calves behind the girth. He may push on the horse's neck to get that first forward step. If the colt fails to respond to these aids, the assistant with the lunge line may ask for the walk, reinforcing the command with the whip if necessary. This procedure is followed for each gait. When the rider feels he has enough control of the colt so that he can guide his

A dropped nose band teaches the colt to relax and flex his neck when bit pressure increases, rather than open his mouth and raise his head.

direction and control his speed, the lunge line can be taken off. This is usually the case after the colt has been ridden for several days.

The trainer must realize that the extra burden of his weight can easily cause a sore back for the colt that has never before been ridden. The mounted sessions should last no longer than five or ten minutes at first, gradually growing longer as the colt becomes used to the rider's weight. It is important to create as little discomfort to the colt as possible because if he associates discomfort with a rider, he will resent his rider and will not give his complete cooperation to him. The trainer must also realize that the colt will have difficulty balancing with a rider on his back and will be most uncoordinated in his movements, especially on small turns. The trainer should try to make large circles and turns until he feels the colt has developed enough balance to decrease the size of the circles and still handle them with agility.

The equipment used on the colt when he is first mounted is very important. The idea is to prevent difficulties from arising instead of allowing them to arise and then curing them. A large mild snaffle bit should be used. A running martingale adjusted to the height of the withers will keep the bit working on the bars of the mouth even when the colt raises his head. An overcheck rein loosely fastened will keep the colt from lowering his head to the point of bucking or pulling. The overcheck is fastened to the pommel of the saddle. The trainer must be alert to the colt's evasions and try to collect them immediately.

A dropped noseband teaches the colt to relax and flex his lower jaw when bit pressure increases rather than to open his mouth and raise his head.

It is a good idea to work the colt alone because his power of concentration will be greater than it would be if he is following another horse. He will have to learn to work independently sometime anyway so he might as well start out that way. Later, when the rider feels he has control of the colt, he should be worked with other horses. He must always follow the rider's commands, however, and not imitate the horse in front of him.

It makes it easy for the colt if he is worked on the lunge line at a walk and trot with the rider on his back for the first time or two. The rider should continue using the voice aids he used when schooling the colt on the lunge line. As he uses his voice, he also applies his rein and leg aids. The colt will learn these aids by a process of association. Having learned the voice aids makes the association very easy for the colt to learn. In fact, it makes the whole process of being trained to ride much easier on the colt.

The rider can ask for the canter from the trot at first, just as he did on the lunge line. The colt should be cantered from a walk only when he is balanced enough and coordinated enough with a rider on his back to accomplish a smooth canter departure. It is important for the rider to stabilize the colt; allowing him to work freely and maintain an even cadence at all three gaits. Only then can he proceed further in his training.

The colt trained to work under English tack should not be inhibited in his movements. He should be allowed to move freely forward. His walk should be alert and lively. His trot should be relaxed and the stride should be long and low. The trainer should work toward a relaxed, confident mount that is well balanced and agile. He should seek cooperation rather than demand it. A colt that enjoys his work progresses rapidly; the colt that has had a few bad experiences in the hands of the trainer will resent his work and will be more difficult. This is not to say that the colt should not be punished for a disobedience. When the colt deliberately misbehaves, he should be punished quickly and sharply with voice or crop. The trainer must be certain he does not ask for more than the colt can give and then become irritated because the colt will not or cannot respond. The trainer must know his horse and proceed with the best methods he knows and not attempt to rush the process.

The trainer must not forget the importance of circles, figure eights, serpentines, and so forth when schooling the colt. The colt should be taught turns on the forehand and turns on the haunches. These exercises help the colt become athletic, agile and responsive. Riders interested in a truly agile, athletic horse should investigate the various dressage exercises which will help to produce a very supple, obedient horse. There are several excellent books on the subject, but the novice dressage rider will need expert help so that he will truly understand the goals of dressage and how to accomplish them.

After the colt is stabilized — willing to work at all three gaits on a loose rein and do so quietly and in a cadenced manner — the trainer may begin working on extended gaits and collection. Stabilizing the colt may take as long as six months to a year, depending on the time spent on his training. The trainer should begin working the colt more and more up into the bit so that he has greater instant control of the horse. The colt will hesitate at first when he feels the pressure from the bit. The rider will have to continue to drive the colt forward with his legs. The colt will be held between the hands and legs. This process of teaching the colt to work on the bit will advance into collection at all three gaits. Collection creates a horse that is working more off his haunches. His body is "shortened" as is his stride. His stride is also more elevated. The horse should work quietly when the rider asks for collection; he should not become excited and anticipate commands. The rider should work the colt in this manner for a short time only at first. It is very tiring because the muscles are strongly used and in a manner to which the horse is not accustomed. The trainer may alternate between collection and free work. The horse should always be warmed up by working freely until the trainer feels he is ready for more strenuous activities.

The extended trot is a gait which most English type horses should be taught to execute. This does not mean a fast trot. It means an *extended* trot. The horse maintains his cadence and rhythm but lengthens his stride to such a degree that the rider can see the horse's legs out in front of him. The feel of this gait is not the same as that of the ordinary trot. The rider feels the lengthening of the stride beneath him. This gait is difficult for the shorter, stockier horses to perform, but with persistence it does eventually come. ■

CHAPTER EIGHT

TRAINING THE HUNTER

A horse should not be schooled over fences until he is four or five years of age because of the softness of his bones and the strong possibility of permanent injury, especially to the front legs. As a two-year old in basic training, the trainer could walk or trot the colt over two by four "logs" so the colt gets used to stepping over obstacles rather than going around them. A series of logs five to six feet apart, depending on the stride of the animal, are good to trot over because they teach the colt to watch where he is going, to look down at obstacles, and to measure his stride. Although this type of exercise is not done every day, it is a good start for the colt who's trainer plans to make a hunter or jumper out of him.

When the colt is three years old, the trainer can begin working over cavalettis that are off the ground about six inches. These can be ten to twelve foot poles (4″ x 4″ with the edges trimmed) set in cement blocks. The colt is asked to trot over these and he is eventually taught to canter over them. The colt learns to canter over one, then two, then three, etc. as he develops his agility. These should be set a canter-stride apart; about twelve feet.

Too many trainers that do not understand how to train a jumper are prematurely anxious to obtain height in the jump. This is incorrect because the horse has to develop confidence in himself over fences before he will jump any obstacle of height. The competent trainer will broaden his jumps rather than raise them. A ground line must be placed in front of the jump so that the horse can judge the height of the jump. If the horse is jumping too late, or taking off too close to the jump, this ground bar can be set in front of the jump a foot or two. The trainer should work the horse over a variety of low, wide jumps and combinations of jumps so that the horse builds confidence in himself. Height will come later. It is important for the trainer to remember not to overdo the jumping. It is a good idea to work the horse on the flat at all three gaits, figures, and so forth. Then school him over cavalettis and low jumps until he is well warmed up and ready to concentrate, or whenever he becomes bored with flat work and needs something more interesting to do. He should not be worked over fences every day — because he may develop a dislike for this

The trainer of the hunter or jumper must have very good hands and balance.

work unless the time over fences is kept minimal. It is important not to tire the horse out when jumping or he will become sloppy and careless. His muscles may get sore and stiff and he will have difficulty jumping. Once the horse is jumping freely over a variety of obstacles two and one half to three feet, the height may be raised.

If the horse refuses to jump a strange obstacle, the jump should be lowered and, in the case of a brush jump or coop, the fearsome object moved off to the side. As the horse jumps the obstacle and begins to lose his fear of it, the fearsome object may be pushed closer to the center of the jump each time the horse goes over the obstacle. Once the horse is jumping freely and without fear, the obstacle may be raised again.

It is important not to punish the horse for each refusal and runout. A horse in training is not too happy about jumping and punishment only adds to his worries. Rather be persistent and patient, and when the horse does respond correctly by jumping the fence he has been refusing, reward him by letting him relax or put him away for the day.

Do not allow the horse to rush the fence. This does not help his

ability to jump at all; rather it causes him to jump wildly and in an

A series of "logs" five to six feet apart, depending on the stride of the animal, are good to trot over because they teach the colt to watch where he is going.

The competent trainer will broaden his jumps rather than raise them. A ground line must be placed in front of the jump to help the horse judge the height.

uncontrollable fashion that is not really safe for the rider. If the horse begins to rush his fences, he should be worked over them at a steady trot as he did in the beginning of his training. The rider may circle him away from the fence he is rushing, or halt him at the fence, ask him to back, then trot a few steps toward the jump. The horse must learn to take the fence in cadence with his stride — no speeding up or slowing down unless the rider distinctly requests it.

The rider must allow the horse to learn to jump by himself. The horse must not depend on the rider for the cue to jump. The horse will learn timing and so forth and thus, in the case of a sticky situation, will take care of himself and his rider and not wait for his rider to get them both out of trouble.

The trainer of the hunter or jumper must have very good hands and balance. He must not accidentally pull on the horse's mouth when the horse is jumping, nor flop down on his back as the horse completes the jump. This punishes the horse and will certainly discourage his desire to jump. Most horses are willing to learn anything the rider attempts to teach. The rider who is unsuccessful should look to himself first because he is quite often unaware of his own limitations as a rider and trainer, and is only too quick to blame the horse. ■

CHAPTER NINE

GROOMING THE HUNTER

Each breed of horse has its own particular method of being groomed and fitted for the show ring; the hunter is no exception. It is important that the show horse wear a blanket most of the time in order to maintain a luxurious, glossy coat. He should not be turned out on pasture during hot, sunny days because his coat will fade and become dull. If he is to be turned out for grass, it should be in the evening after the sun has gone down.

When clipping the hunter, a very small area behind the ears, known as the bridle path, may be prepared so that the halter and bridle will look neater — no hairs will be rubbed and unruly. Other breeds clip a larger bridle path area to create the effect of a slender throat latch. The hunter often has no bridle path area clipped but, if his owner prefers, it should be a very small, unnoticeable area.

The inside of the ear is clipped for neatness. Chin and excess facial hair is clipped again for a neater appearance. The fetlock hair is clipped. The mane and forelock are never cut with scissors to obtain the short appearance. They are pulled. This is done with the help of a pulling comb if one is available, or the fingers can be used if one does not have a comb. The mane is back-combed and the remainder of the hairs are wrapped around the comb and pulled out, or merely pulled out by hand. This not only shortens the mane, it thins it. The mane is pulled to about two to three inches. This is a good length for braiding.

The hunter's mane and forelock are braided for the show ring. The braids should be small and neatly done. The mane is combed thoroughly and wet down with a brush. The "groom" braids a section about an inch to an inch and a half. When he reaches the limit of the braid he runs a needle with a knotted piece of heavy black (or matching color) thread through the lower end of the braid. He winds this around the end of the braid and sews it through several times. He next loops the braid under and sews this tightly. If the mane is a little long or the groom prefers a short braid, he may roll the braid to the desired length and then sew it. Rubber bands or yarn may be used, but sewing is neater and less obvious.

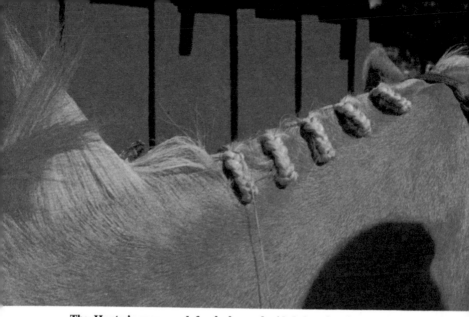

The Hunter's mane and forelock are braided for the show-ring. The braids should be neatly done, consisting of a section of mane about an inch and a half wide.

The tail should also be braided. This is done in a French braid, picking up the hairs along the side all the way down to the end of the tail bone.

The tail should also be braided. This is done in a French braid, picking up the hairs along the side as the groom braids down to the end of the tail bone. At the end, he may again sew the braid, or fasten it with a rubber band. This pigtail is tucked up under the French braid and fastened so that a small loop is the only part of the pigtail that is obvious.

The hunter should present a neat, workmanlike appearance in the show ring. Cleanliness is all important as is neatness of grooming and braiding. The time spent on this chore is necessary for successful competition. ■

CHAPTER TEN

GROOMING THE AMERICAN SADDLE HORSE

The horse which is ridden Saddle Seat is groomed and outfitted differently than the hunter. The hunter is a working horse. The Saddle Horse is a glamorous "peacock." He is decorated rather than groomed. The feet are allowed to grow to lengths unsuitable to any terrain except that of the show ring. To these feet add weighted shoes, and the horse becomes a high-stepping, "showy" animal.

The three gaited horse (or walk-trot horse) is shown with his mane and forelock roached, or shaved off. A few inches down the dock of the tail are also shaved. The ears are trimmed out and the chin whiskers and fetlock hair are removed. The show horse is usually kept blanketed at all times and will wear a tail-set in order to create the high tail carriage.

The five gaited horse wears a full mane and tail but his forelock and the first lock of mane hair are braided with ribbons suitable to the horse's color. The bridle path is trimmed a good way back in order to present a longer and more elegant neck, as well as a clean throat latch.

The American Saddlebred pleasure horse is shown with a full mane and tail. He does not have a set tail. He may or may not be braided. His feet are shod naturally as one would for the trail.

The Arabian shown Saddle Seat is neatly clipped with a bridle path of up to four inches, but has a natural foot and is not braided. This also applies to the Morgan horse shown this way, but they do have a more exaggerated manner of shoeing than the Arabian. Morgans as well as American Saddle Horses are often shod for high action, depending on the classes in which they are shown.

The horse's feet should be kept dressed with a preparation which adds moisture to the hoof. This also aids in the general appearance to the hoof when showing. Hoof preparations now on the market are non-drying and excellent for the show ring as they put a finishing touch on the entire grooming process. ■

The five-gaited horse wears a full mane and tail, but his forelock and the first lock of mane hair are braided with ribbons suitable to the color of the horse.

The Arabian shown Saddle Seat is neatly clipped with a bridle path of up to four inches, but has a natural foot and is not braided.

CONCLUSION

It must be evident to all readers that horses, although not machines, certainly do have "controls." While these controls might not come neatly labeled and identifiable as such by use of an owner's manual, they are there nevertheless.

We have reinforced our previous knowledge that these controls do not begin simply with a loudly bellowed "Giddyap!" . . . and a kick of the heels, then terminated with a jerk on the reins and a screeched "Whoa!" Controlling a horse depends upon communication between rider and horse, and the lines of communication must extend in both directions. A good rider should be able to anticipate what his horse is going to do a second or two before he does it, just as much as he needs to communicate to the horse that he wants him to do something a split-second *before* he asks him to do it.

"English" riding represents a tremendously versatile kind of horsemanship. A great variety of equipment, including the use of double bits and reins, affords a wide range of control not completely provided in most other forms of riding. These advanced controls culminate in the gymnastic exercises known as dressage, the classical form of which is best represented by the Spanish Riding School of Austria — a skill bordering on art, and a joy to all horsemen who have witnessed it.

Who is to say that the symphonic conductor produces the greatest music in the world, for there are those who might opt for guitars and vocal groups. One thing is for sure — the symphonic conductor controls a greater range of instruments, inflections and moods, and the enduring quality of his musical product attests to the validity of his musicianship.

So it is with the accomplished "English" rider! ■